JOEY

A Little Owl Book Holt, Rinehart and Winston, Inc., New York

KANGAROO

by Patricia K. Miller and Iran L. Seligman

Illustrations by Ed Renfro

Copyright © 1963 by Holt, Rinehart and Winston, Inc.
Library of Congress Catalog Card Number 63-17246
Printed in the United States of America
All rights reserved.
4-9770-1513

Pockets! Pockets! Pockets!

Here is another pocket. Do you know
what is in it? It is a baby kangaroo.
All baby kangaroos are called joeys.
The mother kangaroo carries her joey
with her.

A baby kangaroo is only one inch long when it is born. It has no fur. It cannot see. As soon as it is born it crawls into the pocket.

The baby kangaroo stays in the pocket for four months. The pocket keeps it safe and warm. The mother makes milk in her body to feed the joey. If you could look in the pocket, you would see how much bigger it is growing.

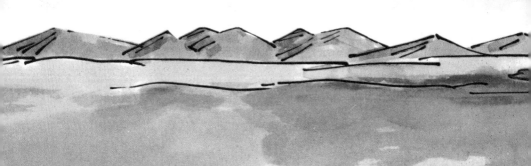

In and out! In and out! Now the joey
can leave the pocket. He comes out to
jump and play. His mother shows him
how to eat grass. Then he goes back into
the pocket.

As the days go by the joey grows
bigger and bigger. One day he tries to
get into the pocket, but he is too big now.
His mother will not let him get in.

Now the joey takes care of himself.
He finds grass to eat. He jumps along
with his mother.

One, two, three, four, five and more.
How many kangaroos do you see with
the joey and his mother?

Kangaroos live together in small groups. A group of kangaroos is called a mob. The strongest male kangaroo is the leader of the mob. He had to fight the other male kangaroos to become the leader. He had to show that he was the strongest kangaroo. He had to show that he could take care of the mob.

Up and down! Up and down! The
kangaroos are jumping to find food.

Kangaroos sleep during the day, and look for food at night. They move together from place to place, looking for food.

Kangaroos eat grass. They nibble leaves from small trees. They eat fruit and vines.

Hop! Hop! Splash! Kangaroos like to play in the water. They like to cuff and box with each other, too.

A kangaroo has a long, heavy tail.
It rests on its tail when it sits. It pushes
with its tail when it jumps. It pushes
down with its tail...and up it goes!
Look how high a kangaroo can jump!

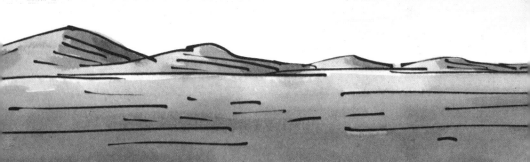

WOMBAT

TREE KANGAROO

Down, down, down and around—all
the way to Australia! That is where
kangaroos live. There are other animals
with pockets that live in Australia. You
can see them on this map. Perhaps some
day you will go to Australia.

KOALA

MARSUPIAL MOUSE

KANGAROO